How To Teach

Cosmetologists & Barbers

To Be

MILLIONAIRES

How To Teach

Cosmetologists & Barbers

To Be

MILLIONAIRES

By: Cuttie W. Bacon III, Ph.D.

Published by:
C.W. Bacon Publications
Chicago, Illinois

**How To Teach
Cosmetologists & Barbers
To Be Millionaires**

By: Cuttie W. Bacon III, Ph.D.

Copyright © MMII

Published by:
C.W. Bacon Publications, Chicago, Illinois

Cover design and page layout by:
Ad Graphics, Inc., Tulsa, OK

Printed in the United States of America

ISBN Number: 0-9678544-2-3

About the Author

Cuttie Bacon was born in Western Kentucky and lived the first four years of his life on a farm where his Father was a farmer. Cuttie Bacon grew up in Louisville, Kentucky where he finished high school and graduated from Kentucky State University. He moved to Chicago where he earned a Master's Degree at Loyola University in Chicago and a Ph.D. at Northwestern University in Evanston, Illinois. Cuttie has taught at Northwestern University, Mundelein College, Governors State University, National College and has led numerous seminars over the past twenty years. His administrative experience in public school started as a Principal and later as a Superintendent of Schools in the Southern Suburbs of Chicago.

Cuttie frequently speaks and runs seminars on personal finance and is an expert in personal finance. He has authored 5 books, *How to Teach*

Kids to Be Millionaires, How to Write and Publish Your Own Book, How to Manage and Build a Beauty Empire, How to Teach College Students to Be Millionaires and *How to Get and Stay out of Bad Debt.*

Cuttie is an entertaining speaker and is able to see the humorous side of life in almost any subject. One of his many hobbies is restoring exotic and antique cars.

Cuttie consistently speaks and gives seminars on the Millionaires Series, Personal Finance and How to Invest. His company is C.W. Bacon Seminars; email him at:

Cuttie3@Compuserve.com

or call toll free, 1-800-955-9934.

Foreword

From his vast experience in the education profession, we get edifying understanding. From his incredible knowledge of how money works, Dr. Cuttie W. Bacon, III has delivered a valuable tool for cosmetologists, barbers, nail technicians and educators in the beauty profession. This book applied and studied systematically will give a change in the consciousness of the beauty business. The cosmetology industry is one of the most underestimated and postulated professions and it is totally indispensable. A recession proof opportunity that allows one to set their schedule and their own income earning potential. In many states this service oriented career encourages entrepreneurship with minute training periods as compared to others with longer term training and the same earning potential.

Upon completing his book *How to Teach Kids to Be Millionaires*, we invited Dr. Bacon to speak to our student body on the topic *How to Teach Cosmetologists & Barbers to Be Millionaires*. His enthusiasm, humor, wit and wisdom were simply exceptional. Some of the students at Dudley Beauty College-Chicago remarked that his message truly changed their perception for their cosmetology future.

Cosmetic professionals that understand and use the methods outlined in Dr. Bacon's book will make an impact on the manner society perceives the industry. These professionals will also value the revenue they generate from their investments.

Thank you Dr. Cuttie Bacon, III for your contribution to the growth and stabilization of the cosmetology industry. Your steps are definitely ordered to help change the world through Cosmetology.

Betty R. Clawson
Dudley Beauty College
School Director

Acknowledgments

To acknowledge all of the sources I consulted with in preparing *How to Teach Cosmetologists & Barbers to Be Millionaires* would be impossible. The inspiration and support in writing this book and putting together the final manuscript was supplied by Juliane Batts who consistently reviewed and encouraged every page. She made certain I met every deadline on time.

I would like to thank Betty R. Clawson for her support, information, and encouragement to complete this book.

I sincerely thank all the people who consistently assured me the book was a good idea and not to stop until I include *How to Teach Cosmetologists & Barbers to Be Millionaires* in my millionaire's series.

Table of Contents

The lack of love can be
the root of all evil.

– Cuttie W. Bacon III, Ph.D.

Introduction

For more than 25 years I have taught entrepreneurship, economics, personal finance and management. I have owned more than six businesses. These experiences along with being a college professor and a seminar leader have allowed me to interact with numerous people and entrepreneurs. During these years I have known many business owners that have made large sums of money and are broke today. These business people tell me if only they had been able to read my books on money and money management, attend some of my seminars, and get the kind of educational information needed to be successful, they would be in a different financial situation today.

I have had several personal friends and relatives who were wealthy from the beauty business; however, because of poor management they were broke ten years later with no resources.

I believe some of the main things missing are education, discipline, good management skills, vision, love for customers, and faith in God. I believe this book can give you significant information on becoming a millionaire.

Chapter 1

How Millionaires Act and Think

Characteristics that most often are displayed by millionaires:

- Strong positive winning attitude.
- Good communication and people skills.
- Honest with all people.
- Have a passion for their business.
- Have unlimited energy.
- Strong leadership skills.
- Great selling skills.
- Have a strong need to give and receive respect.
- Have a need to be their own boss.
- Not afraid to take risks.
- Have good organization skills.
- Work harder and longer than most people.

- See money making opportunities that others do not.

- Have strong spiritual relationships.

- Put God or a superior being first, family second, business third.

- Usually live below their means.

In thinking and acting like a millionaire and as a professional in the beauty and barber industry, you must always be aware that you are viewed as an expert in your field. Because you are looked upon as a professional, having a beautiful attitude is most important. A beautiful attitude means that no matter what time of the day or your personal situation, the only thing you show is a genuine positive and caring attitude for everyone you encounter.

Appearance

Your appearance everyday and every hour of the day should be that of beauty. That means from your head to your toe you should display well groomed hair, well groomed makeup and a total appearance of I am a millionaire and I am prosperous.

Thought Processes

To make sure your appearance is what you want it to be develop and control the words you use and the thoughts you have in your own mind. Always think positive and how much better you can help clients look and feel, as a result of their being in your care, for the time they spend with you.

Professionalism

As a professional, the number one thing you have to offer every client is service with a smile. Show love with a smile and caring with a smile. Before you can offer love, caring and superior service to your customer you must first love yourself. Loving yourself may mean working on yourself and getting help through professional services and reading how to truly love oneself.

The following is a self-questionnaire to inventory yourself and to determine if you truly love yourself:

Question 1: Do I look my best at all times?
Yes or No

Question 2: Do I speak using the best words that I can possibly use at all times?

Yes or No

Question 3: Do I use profanity when I speak to others?

Yes or No

Question 4: Do I have good things to say about anybody and everybody that I meet or know?

Yes or No

Question 5: Am I envious of people who have things that I don't have?

Yes or No

Question 6: Do I blame other people for my lack of success?

Yes or No

Question 7: Do I consume illegal drugs?

Yes or No

Question 8: Do I forgive myself easily when I screw up?

Yes or No

Question 9: Do I only consume healthy foods?
Yes or No

Question 10: Do I treat everybody like I want to be treated?
Yes or No

I am rich
In soul and mind.
I am a professional
Sharing and kind.
I'm clean and meticulous,
Manage money with care,
Who am I?
I'm a millionaire.

– Cuttie W. Bacon III, Ph.D.

Chapter 2

How to Work Your Plan

L ike taking a trip across the country, it is necessary when you start in business to have a plan. The plan does not have to be a long detailed one, but it is my recommendation that first you start with a daily plan, a weekly plan, a monthly plan, a yearly plan, and a five year plan. Whether you are already in business now or plan to go into the beauty business, if you do not have a plan, here are some recommendations.

Take a notebook and decide how many hours of work per day you plan to work. To get started use the space provided on pages 75 – 79.

- How many clients you plan to serve per day?

- How much product you plan to sell everyday?

- How much time you will set aside for reading, for sleeping, for exercise, prayer and meditation?

- Time with your spouse or significant other and children?
- Social and recreational time?

Notice I did not include time to gossip. Count that out of your day, your week, your month, your year, and your life.

Your weekly plan should include,

- bookkeeping
- self-improvement
- reading
- taking courses
- ordering products
- keeping an inventory
- depositing daily receipts
- advertisement
- evaluation and reflection of services to clients
- developing new ways to increase your clientele

Include the following in your monthly plan,

- Meeting with an accountant or bookkeeper
- Paying monthly bills

- Developing and creating monthly promotions for your business
- Sending birthday cards to clients
- Attending educational and product conferences and seminars
- Reviewing monthly plans and goals

Yearly Goals

- Yearly reviewing whether or not you accomplished your goals
- Filing Federal, State and local taxes
- Renewing licenses
- Reviewing yearly goals and making new goals and plans for the new year

Following the daily, weekly, monthly and yearly plans which I have talked about, it is advisable after one year to plan to own your own salon. After one year you can have additional beauty care staff to work with you or for you in a full service salon and spa. After establishing your own full service salon and spa your goal should be to own several facilities and no longer work from behind the chair but from behind your desk chair and your home to become a multi-millionaire.

So I won't lose friends
I never lend (money).
I don't like sorrow
So I don't let friends
Borrow (money).

– Cuttie W. Bacon III, Ph.D.

Chapter 3

You Are the Last to Get Paid

*You should make the money
before you spend it.*

One of the hardest concepts I had to learn was managing daily cash flow. When you finish services to a client you are generally paid in cash. Many operators that receive cash that goes in their pocket or in a cash register find it is far too easy to begin spending the money within minutes or seconds after receiving it. Here is one of the most comical scenarios my significant other told me a few days ago. She was having her hair shampooed at her favorite hairstylist. Her hair was wet and dripping with shampoo. Her stylist asked her if she could pay her because a friend was going next door to get a Polish sausage and French-fries.

I bring this story as humor but it is told to illustrate that as a professional, care has to be demonstrated in handling and spending the cash you receive on a daily basis.

The following are examples of what a professional's expenses are when they receive $600 per day on a typical day.

- Rent per day: $25

- Supplies: $60

- Payments on equipment: $10

- Uniforms: $5

- Federal Taxes: $30

- State taxes: $10

- SSI: $10

- Medicare: $3

- Insurance: $5

- Advertisement: $5

- Miscellaneous: $37

- Salary: $300

Total Estimated Expenses: $500

- The total typical expenses to take in $600 per day would total $500.

- Without any unforeseen expectancies, your gross profit is $100 per day.

- No longer can you spend as if you receive $600 per day.

- After your expenses, you only have approximately $100.

- The $600 per day is called your *gross earnings.*

- The $100 is known as your *net earnings.*

- From this point forward, refer to the amount in your cash register as your gross earnings that belongs to your business.

- Your income for that day is $100.

- In order to avoid overspending and getting in credit trouble, pay yourself approximately $300 per day.

- Work on plans to double your daily income from a $600 per day gross to a $1,200 per day gross so that you can begin to accumulate the wealth you have been dreaming of to become a millionaire.

- Invest $200 per week at 8% interest or more interest and you will have one million in less than 20 years.

A Word on Taxes and Expenses

The Departments of Treasury and Internal Revenue Services enforce federal laws that state if you are self-employed, you owe taxes on your income. Failure to pay such taxes makes you subject to penalties and fines and/or imprisonment for income tax evasion.

There are several recommendations that I would make to avoid complications from not paying taxes.

- Study the Internal Revenue Publications 535 and 463. Both give you the basic rules on business expenses, travel, entertainment, gifts, and car expenses.

- Get the service of a good certified public accountant that has the experience of working with beauty professionals.

- Make certain you keep accurate records of receipts on <u>everything</u> on a day-to-day basis.

- Remember most of the time more than half of the money that you receive from a client is consumed in the expenses for rent, supplies and all of the expenses that go into doing business.

- Setting up your books with a professional certified public account, keeping good records and receipts, and knowing the rules of Internal Revenue, State Revenue and Social Security can save you a number of headaches and problems in the future.

You're the last to get paid
It's painful but true,
Pay suppliers,
Pay utilities,
These are only a few.
You're a talented professional
You create beautiful hair,
But manage profits wisely
To become a millionaire.

– Cuttie W. Bacon III, Ph.D.

Chapter 4

Put Yourself on a Weekly Salary

Putting yourself on a weekly salary will enable you to see yourself as an employee of your business and to avoid paying yourself or spending money out of your daily receipts. Paying yourself a weekly salary is important because one of the worst practices beauty professionals have is spending money out of their cash register on a daily and hourly basis. Having a weekly salary allows you to take care of your personal needs with cash from your business and not confuse your business money with your personal money. In short, it makes your budgeting simple.

Pitfalls or problems when you don't give yourself a weekly salary

In a typical salon or shop, there are 50 opportunities a day to spend money out of your cash register. This can lead to trouble if you have not set aside money for your daily and personal use.

- Many professionals start their day out with coffee and breakfast. That can be $5–$10 out of your cash register.

- Peddlers selling purses, watches, jewelry earrings, scarves can tempt you to spend an approximate $25 per day.

- Cigarettes, soft drinks, coffee and snacks can total $10 per day.

- Parking your car $10 per day.

- Lunch $8–$10 per day.

- Loan to coworker $10.

- Dinner $10–$15.

- Gasoline for your car $15.

- Snack on the way to work $5.

As you can see it is very easy to spend $100 per day if you are not keeping track of what you are doing and if you are not keeping track of your daily receipts. Some operators have reported they have spent up to $300 in one day out of their $600 gross. The danger in spending your daily receipts means that you are spending more than your profits and you will never realize wealth accumulation and money in the bank.

The solution is,

pay yourself a salary,

budget your daily spending, and

watch yourself grow rich!

Spend your money slow
Your finances will grow.
Spend your money fast,
Prosperity won't last.
You've worked hard
For every dollar,
Budget money with care.
Nothing can stop you
From becoming a millionaire.

– Cuttie W. Bacon III, Ph.D.

Chapter 5

Paying Taxes Is a Must

*The old saying is that two things you must do
sooner or later is pay taxes and die*

Most people think they will live forever. Many self-employed people, like people in the beauty profession, believe that somehow they should not have to pay taxes. Some believe they can get away without paying taxes. I must acknowledge that I have met a few people that for considerably long periods of time have been able to get around not paying taxes. The tragedy is, once Uncle Sam catches up with you, Uncle Sam wants everything. When penalties are added to the taxes you owe, that amount is doubled, tripled or quadrupled. When you do not have accurate records to show your actual expenses and profits and what you owe, the Internal Revenue decides for you what you owe in taxes.

An acquaintance of mine that was a very successful product manufacturer earned millions of dollars. Enough to have more than $5 million dollars in houses, more than a dozen luxury automobiles, and anything any man could ever dream of. He ended in tax court for not paying his taxes. Due to the high cost of accountants and lawyers, a man who at one time was grossing more than $25 million a year ended up near broke. The main reason he did not go to jail was he had a reputation of giving freely and knew plenty of people that spoke highly of him. As a result, the courts did not send him to prison and had mercy on him.

In yet another case, a salon owner went for more than ten years without paying taxes and was finally caught. The Internal Revenue totaled up the cost of his automobiles, clothing, jewelry, and house payments. The IRS determined that he had been making more $150,000 per year and had a tax liability with penalties of more than a half million dollars. All of his properties and cars were auctioned off. His diamond rings, furs, and all assets were sold. He still owes Uncle Sam. I say this not to frighten you but to alert you that **taxes must be paid.**

There are a number of tax loop-holes and laws that allow practically everything business related to your business to be deducted from your gross receipts. Employ a good certified public accountant. Follow their advise and the tax laws and you can avoid the pitfalls and headaches that many people have made because they thought they could survive without paying taxes.

It is possible to have a gross income of a half million dollars or more and have business expenses that exceed your gross income. With correct bookkeeping and filing your taxes correctly with a certified public account, you may end up owing little or no taxes. However, not filing your taxes and not using proper bookkeeping and assuming you can get away without paying taxes is business suicide.

Learn the tax laws
And you'll know what's required
To pay Uncle Sam
And by the time you're retired
You are living comfortably
On the nest egg you prepare,
You are now on the road
To becoming a millionaire.

– Cuttie W. Bacon III, Ph.D.

Chapter 6

How to Buy a Salon

After renting space or a location to conduct your business for a year or more, a beauty professional should consider owning their own salon or shop. I would recommend buying a salon that you can afford within the income and money that you feel fairly certain that you can generate.

Obviously any investment involves some risk. However, if you have been in the business for a year or more and if you have successfully paid rent of $100+ per week, remember that you along with two other people paying $100 per week equal more that $15,000 per year. Fifteen thousand dollars is the approximate payment on a property that costs from $150,000 – $175,000 dollars.

Plan big.
Succeed big.
No plan is too big.

– Cuttie W. Bacon III, Ph.D.

Advantages of Owning Your Own Salon and Shop

A salon costing $150,000 – $175,000 could be paid in full within ten years. You can plan that after ten years you will be able to increase the gross income by more than $15,000 per year. If you purchase property in the right locations and property continues to appreciate, in ten years instead of being worth $150,000 it can be worth $300,000. In yet another ten years if it doubles, it can be worth a half million dollars or more.

Owning our own property elevates your professional reputation and gives you a stable and consistent location.

There are many other advantages and some disadvantages to owning your salon. The advantages far outweigh the disadvantages. The advantages so far outweigh the disadvantages so, as Grandpa would say, "it would not take a rocket scientist" to know that one should own their own salon or shop.

You need a shop of your own
Where you are in charge,
You are ready
You have earned it,
Open small
Grow to large.
Property value will grow
Select with care,
Location is essential
For a millionaire.

– Cuttie W. Bacon III, Ph.D.

Chapter 7

How to Buy a Home

Buying a home has some of the same advantages to accumulating wealth as buying a salon. First let me give you a personal experience with buying houses and condos in my life. Fifteen years ago I purchased a condominium for $31,000 in one of the middle income very stable neighborhoods of Chicago. In less than ten years it was appraised at $65,000. Today after 15 years of ownership the property is now worth $110,000.

Less than seven years ago, I purchased another condo for a little more than $100,000. Today it is worth more than $200,000.

There are advantages in purchasing property in the right location. If you have a good location it is common for property to double in value in ten or less years.

The advantage of buying a home to live in is your mortgage payments do not increase each year like rent. The first house I bought had a mortgage of less than $250 per month. My payments were the same after 20 years. An apartment in the same location that would rent for $250 per month 20 years ago now rents for $1,250. By purchasing a house or condo one could be saving as much as $1,000 – $2000 per month in 20 years.

When purchasing a house, acquire a 15 year mortgage and try to pay the mortgage off in 7 or less years. You will save thousands of dollars.

There are three things you need to remember in determining where to buy a house or a condo.

They are,

location,

location,

location.

A 2 bedroom house in the right location in Hollywood, California may sell for $2 million. The same house in Gary, Indiana may sell for $20,000. Remember location, location, location.

Today buying a house is easier than it has ever been in the history of our country. There are numerous no money down houses available. There are houses with 5% or 10% percent down and programs to give you a portion of the down payment.

Many people can buy a house for the same amount of money they are paying for rent.

My home is my castle,
I'm the King
I'm the Queen,
I'm the Lord and the Master
(You know what I mean).
Everything about me is regal
I hold my head high in the air,
I present myself always
Like a millionaire.

– Cuttie W. Bacon III, Ph.D.

Chapter 8

How to Buy Clothing and Jewelry Like a Millionaire

As you study the lifestyles of most millionaires like those described in the *Millionaire Next Door* book, you will find that most millionaires when surveyed are not known to buy an abundance of expensive designer's clothing, expensive furs, and wearing apparel. People often ask why millionaires who can well afford to buy any kind of clothes at any price choose to buy moderately priced clothing.

In discussing these practices with a few millionaires and other wealthy people, it became very clear to me that people who have high self esteem and know who they are have no need to buy expensive clothing and wearing apparel to impress people. As one barber who is obviously wealthy put it, "Six days a week, twelve hours a day I wear a uniform. I only have one day without a uniform. On the one or two occasions a week that I do go somewhere I need something other than my uniform or ordinary clothing."

He went on to further state that he needed about six good outfits and work clothing. The reason why he did not spend lots of money on designer's and expensive clothing is; (1) He never got around to wearing them, and (2) He was successful and he knew that he could buy any kind of clothing and wearing apparel and there was no need to waste money, and (3) He knew that designer's clothing had a markup rate of 500 – 1000%. In other words, a suit that sells for as much as $1,000 from some of the top designers only cost $150 – $200 wholesale. He considered buying $1000 – $2000 suits a waste of money.

Follow the practices of millionaires and buy good moderate priced clothing and invest and save the rest of the money and grow rich.

How to Buy Jewelry

With jewelry, unlike clothing, the markup is even more ridiculous. Many diamond rings at your local jewelry stores that sell for as much as

$2,000 – $3,000 will not yield 20% of their cost at your local jewelry pawn shop. You will be lucky to get $300.

Remember a piece of gold jewelry, bracelet, medallion or platinum jewelry is never worth more than what you would pay for a raw ounce of gold or platinum. For example, recently gold has been advertised as selling for approximately $280 an ounce. If you buy a bracelet that weighs 2 ounces, its true value is $560 even though you may pay as much as $2000 for the bracelet. The true value is the value of its gold. Check your daily papers when you decide to buy gold jewelry. Pay only a few dollars more or less than the price of gold per ounce. Otherwise, it is **not a good buy.**

No one can style hair
As well as I,
I can cut and condition
I can perm, tint and dye.
My clothing is a reflection
Of my multi-talent and skill,
I look like a millionaire
I've climbed to the top of the hill.

– Cuttie W. Bacon III, Ph.D.

Chapter 9

How to Buy a Car and Not Get Ripped Off

One of the biggest items that beauty professionals find themselves buying are cars. Because cars have been used as a sign of wealth, prosperity, success and status many business people find themselves purchasing expensive luxury cars and RVs that they cannot afford.

I have purchased more than 50 cars and presently own five automobiles, I have become an expert through my association with a number of car dealers and brokers and doing extensive research on buying automobiles. It is very clear to me that a new luxury American car and some foreign cars can be one of the worst investments you can make with your money. It can be one of the worst investments because most $50,000 cars will be worth less than $25,000 when 2 years old. This simply means that of all of the $50,000 or more items that you could purchase with your money, the one with the highest rate of depreciation is a new luxury car. That is why I have concluded that buying a new luxury automobile is a very poor investment.

The question is, then what is considered a good buy if you want a luxury, expensive, beautiful automobile?

My advice is always buy a car after it depreciates a year or more. The first year or two it depreciates 20% – 50%. That means you can have the pleasure of driving a two year old luxury car and paying half of what you would ordinarily pay when the car was new.

For a few hundred dollars extra, buy a maintenance agreement as insurance to guard against you getting stuck with a lemon. If you encounter any mechanical deficiencies the car can be fixed without any additional expense to you.

In buying a used car, you may be paying only $25,000 for a car that would ordinarily sell for $50,000. Invest the $25,000 at 8% – 15% and it will double every 4 – 8 years in value and assist you in becoming a millionaire.

Keep in mind when buying a car,

1. The primary reason to own a car is to travel from point "A" to point "B." Any car can accomplish this task.

2. The car does not make you. You make the car.

3. Millionaires for the most part do not drive large new luxury cars.

4. Millionaires generally do not care what kind of car they drive as long as it runs.

5. If your spouse or significant other insists on you driving a new luxurious expensive car, insist on them buying it for you and invest all of your money in stocks, bonds, securities, real estate and mutual funds.

You are now on the road to becoming a millionaire.

Before purchasing a vehicle
To take you about,
Don't put down a penny
Without checking it out.
What's the mileage?
How's the body?
What do the maintenance
Records show?
If you want to be a millionaire
These things you must know.

– Cuttie W. Bacon III, Ph.D.

Chapter 10

Insurance Is a Must

You are in business for yourself. There are risks in any service business.

It is a must to have insurance to cover yourself both professionally and personally.

- Liability insurance is a must to protect against any lawsuits in case you are sued for damages or accidents in your business. Health and accident insurance is also a requirement in case you are hospitalized and unable to work.

- Disability insurance and business interruption insurance will give you an income in case you are disabled or are too ill to work for a considerable amount of time.

- Liability or collision automobile insurance is required in most states by law.

No matter how little
Money you make
Someone is always
On the take.
Insure so you
Won't get the rake.

– Cuttie W. Bacon III, Ph.D.

- Medical and Dental insurance.

- Business content insurance and property insurance for your business and for your home.

Insurance is a must. Nothing can be more catastrophic than having a loss or an accident. This could bankrupt you or cause you to lose or forfeit your business and all your money. The risk of this unfortunate situation can be eliminated with a few dollars or more worth of insurance premiums per month.

See my book *From the Beauty and Barber Shop to the Beauty CEO* for details on this subject.

Keep in mind that when you own your own business people perceive you as having money. A disgruntled client who has an accident or has a skin rash that may or may not have been caused by your product or services, may decide to sue you. Your only protection is to have insurance to protect you against judgments in court.

Insure yourself and insure yourself well. You will not end up being vulnerable for lawsuits.

Protect what you've acquired
Insure what you own,
Your salon and equipment
Your furniture, your home.
Prepare yourself for setbacks
That you cannot prevent,
A millionaire must
Have protection,
Against unexpected events.

— Cuttie W. Bacon III, Ph.D.

Chapter 11

Retirement Plans

At some point in your career either through burn out or old age you probably will decide that you no longer want to work. Generally, that is somewhere between 55 – 65 years of age. In order to retire comfortably and have money to live the lifestyle that you are accustomed, it is necessary to invest money in a retirement program so you will have income to live on after your working days. There are huge numbers of different plans and investments to enable you to successfully retire as you approach retirement.

Some of the more popular known plans are,

- Individual Retirement plans,
- Roth Individual Retirement plans,
- 401K plans,
- Annuities

Retirement plans are too numerous to go into detail, I recommend to all self employed professionals to set aside 10% of their weekly earnings in a retirement fund. I am not an expert on retirement funds so I encourage you to research it and make a decision yourself.

I would recommend that you put your money in a Roth IRA (short for a Roth Individual Retirement Account). Roth IRAs were created by an act of Congress in 1996. In a Roth IRA your money can grow income tax free. When you retire and withdraw your money from a Roth IRA you will not owe any taxes on the money no matter how much the money has grown if you have followed the Internal Revenue Guidelines. In a Roth IRA you can also withdraw your money at any time without any penalties or taxes regardless of how long the money has been in the account. The only money that can be taxed is your earnings. If you leave your money in your Roth IRA account until you are 59 $\frac{1}{2}$ years old and it has been in the account for five years after you retire, you do not have to pay any taxes or penalties. Any single person with an adjusted gross income of less than $95,000 per year can put in up to $2,000 per year. A married couple with an adjusted gross income of $150,000 per year can put in up to $1,000 per year as a single person and married people can put in $1,000 dollars each.

You can participate in both a Roth IRA and a 401K plan if you meet the income qualifications. You can also borrow at a low interest rate on your Roth IRA account and not withdraw any of the funds before retirement. As I discussed earlier, there are numerous pension plans available. Consult a financial advisor or planner on the numerous pension plans that are available.

For more information on Roth IRAs go to: www.mutual-funds-investing.com/roth_ira.asp

There is no plan
To have that's greater,
Than saving now
To have money later.
A millionaire acquires money
From lessons that
Have been learned
And saving 10 percent
Of every dollar earned.

– Cuttie W. Bacon III, Ph.D.

Chapter 12

Planning Your Business Future

*The secret to success is simple.
Give people more than they expect,
and do it with a smile.*

Beauty/Barber Renting a Space

Buying a Salon or Shop

Step 1: All employees on commission.

Step 2: Leasing five spaces.

Step 3: Expanding your business to ten professionals and hiring a manager to run your business.

Step 4: Opening a second salon with ten operators and hiring a manager to run it.

Most people don't fail;
Most people fail to plan.

– Cuttie W. Bacon III, Ph.D.

Step 5: Developing a salon franchise and selling franchises.

Step 6: Developing and marketing your own line of products.

Step 7: Developing a college or university to teach all phases of the beauty industry and hiring a director to run your total Beauty or Barber College or University.

Step 8: Develop a Research and Development center to improve and develop products and advance professional and educational knowledge developing new and improved products.

Step 9: Developing a CEO to run your total operation. Removing yourself from daily operations and diversifying your investment portfolio into other businesses and investments.

This is an example of how you can develop a business. These are steps to follow, not necessarily sequentially, but developmental areas to consider in planning a multi-million dollar and possibly a billion dollar operation.

The future of your business
Is all in your hands,
How hard you work
How smart you budget
How wise you invest
How carefully you plan.

– Cuttie W. Bacon III, Ph.D.

Chapter 13

Tithing, Giving and Prospering

Love is the greatest investment.
No matter who you give it to.

The most rewarding thing you can do as you climb the ladder of success in becoming a millionaire is giving. It is far more rewarding and far more fulfilling to give than to receive. Look for opportunities to give and to give unconditionally.

It is great advertisement to give small items such as key chains, ballpoint pens, and other inexpensive items with your business name and phone number. It is not only good advertisement but good business. One of the noticeable things I have observed in studying the lives of highly successful people in the hair care and product business is studying the life of the wealthy Joe Dudley Sr., President and CEO of Dudley products in North Carolina. Mr. Dudley gives away millions of dollars a year to educate more than 35 college students and contributes generously to other charities. In studying Mr. Dudley's life, he is constantly giving, teaching and showing people how to have a successful business and how to get the educational skills to be successful hair care and beauty professionals. It is obvious that his practice of giving and tithing has a direct relationship with his ability to succeed and have a business empire that earns millions of dollars per year. Using Mr. Dudley as an example, it should be an inspiration to anyone who is pursuing a career as a beauty professional.

We have numerous examples, like Mr. Dudley, whose philosophy and practice of giving, helping others and sharing allowed them to take a few dollars and build a multi-million dollar industry.

Study the lives of millionaires as you start on your journey to wealth. Read and use these fantastic examples of giving. Tithe 10% of your income. Prosper and become another wonderful example of what men and women can do in your profession.

Become a national example of a successful millionaire.

Give unselfishly in
Everything you do,
Generosity is like
A boomerang
It will come back to you.

- Cuttie W. Bacon III, Ph.D.

Chapter 14

Love

- Love is in you.

- Love will solve your business problems.

- Love can promote your business.

- Love will solve your client problems.

- Love will bring prosperity to your life.

- Love will bring success to your life.

- Love will work miracles in your life.

- Love will allow you to always forgive and forgive and forgive.

- Love will never fail.

When you put God first you will open doors. The power of love is the way to increase your financial well being and abundance of everything you need and want in your life. Never forget you were put here to love and to have an abundance of everything.

Don't settle for anything less.

Order Information

To order more copies of this book or receive other products by Cuttie W. Bacon III, Ph.D., contact Dr. Bacon by calling toll free 1-800-955-9934, write him at P.O. Box 81465, Chicago, IL 60681, or e-mail at cuttie3@compuserve.com.

How to Teach Cosmetologists & Barbers to Be Millionaires is a trademark of C. W. Bacon Publications.

* * * * *

To have Dr. Bacon speak to your organization or to order any of his other products contact:

C.W. Bacon Seminars:
Call 1-800-955-9934

or write him at:
P.O. Box 81465, Chicago, IL 60681

or e-mail at:
Cuttie3@compuserve.com

Dr. Bacon will be happy to provide
personal financial consultation to you
or your group. For more information:

Call
1-800-955-9934

or e-mail at
cuttie3@compuserve.com

*Additional help is only
a phone call away.*

Daily Plan

Weekly Plan

Monthly Plan

Yearly Plan

Five Year Plan